F

MW01089151

Memorize Music

Your Step by Step Guide to
Memorizing Music

HowExpert

**For more tips related to this topic, visit
HowExpert.com/memorizemusic.**

Recommended Resources

- HowExpert.com – Quick 'How To' Guides on All Topics from A to Z by Everyday Experts.
- HowExpert.com/free – Free HowExpert Email Newsletter.
- HowExpert.com/books – HowExpert Books
- HowExpert.com/courses – HowExpert Courses
- HowExpert.com/clothing – HowExpert Clothing
- HowExpert.com/membership – HowExpert Membership Site
- HowExpert.com/affiliates – HowExpert Affiliate Program
- HowExpert.com/writers – Write About Your #1 Passion/Knowledge/Expertise & Become a HowExpert Author.
- HowExpert.com/resources – Additional HowExpert Recommended Resources
- YouTube.com/HowExpert – Subscribe to HowExpert YouTube.
- Instagram.com/HowExpert – Follow HowExpert on Instagram.
- Facebook.com/HowExpert – Follow HowExpert on Facebook.

Publisher's Foreword

Dear HowExpert reader,

HowExpert publishes quick 'how to' guides on all topics from A to Z by everyday experts.

At HowExpert, our mission is to discover, empower, and maximize talents of everyday people to ultimately make a positive impact in the world for all topics from A to Z...one everyday expert at a time!

All of our HowExpert guides are written by everyday people just like you and me who have a passion, knowledge, and expertise for a specific topic.

We take great pride in selecting everyday experts who have a passion, great writing skills, and knowledge about a topic that they love to be able to teach you about the topic you are also passionate about and eager to learn about.

We hope you get a lot of value from our HowExpert guides and it can make a positive impact in your life in some kind of way. All of our readers including you altogether help us continue living our mission of making a positive impact in the world for all spheres of influences from A to Z.

If you enjoyed one of our HowExpert guides, then please take a moment to send us your feedback from wherever you got this book.

Thank you and we wish you all the best in all aspects of life.

Sincerely,

BJ Min
Founder & Publisher of HowExpert
HowExpert.com

PS...If you are also interested in becoming a HowExpert author, then please visit our website at HowExpert.com/writers. Thank you & again, all the best!

Table of Contents

Introduction

Why Play Music from Memory?

There are a number of reasons to play music from memory. You might choose to play from memory simply because of things that can unexpectedly go awry when you rely on printed music - You forget your music at home; The music falls off the stand while you're playing; The pages get out of order; Your stand light goes out and you can't see the page. Any of these would be tremendously irritating, might derail your performance, and could be avoided if you memorized the music.

Some deeper and more compelling reasons to memorize have to do with musicality. First, memorizing a piece forces you to *really* learn it. You have to be aware of every detail of performance at all times: notes, rhythms, articulations, dynamics, phrasing, fingering, and everything other aspect of the music. Memorizing forces you to understand your piece in a way that you don't really have to when you sinply read off the page.

Performing without a score is very empowering and liberating. You can move, face your audience, or even play with your eyes closed. Most importantly, the creation of your sound is more organic. It comes directly from you instead of being prompted by dots on paper. Even if you still perform with the score in front of you, knowing that you have the piece memorized is an unparalleled confidence booster.

Finally, memorizing music is a different skill from playing off of a score. Learning to do something new, no matter what it is, will always make you a better, more versatile musician. Therefore, gaining the ability to memorize is a valid personal educational goal, even if you never perform from memory.

There is no single step-by-step process for learning to memorize music that will work for everybody. Each person's brain works differently; every musician has different strengths. This guide is designed to provide a variety of tips and methods, so that you can try them all and decide what works well for you.

How to Use This Guide

DO read through the entire guide once before you start the exercises. Try to gain perspective on the task you are setting out to do.

DO try each exercise at least a couple of times. Something that you didn't think would work might actually be a good methodl for you, once you get used to it.

DON'T feel compelled to implement each and every method fully. Some methods will just "click" and will really help your brain memorize faster; other methods may be ineffective or even frustrating for you. Everybody memorizes differently. Be aware of what works for you and what doesn't.

DO keep a practice log where you detail what you work on each day and how much you accomplish. Make a note of which exercises you tried and what you think of them. This can be very helpful so you can see your progress over time.

DO make a plan for memorization, setting short-term and long-term goals. Organize your work. A practice log can also be a great tool in this regard, as well. Regularly assess whether you are still on track to achieving the goals you have set.

DON'T be rigid about your plan. If a method you are using is not working, scrap it and try a different one.

DON'T get discouraged! Playing music from memory is a complex intellectual task. Just like playing an instrument, it takes a long, long time and a whole lot of patience to master it. The more music you memorize, the easier it becomes to memorize the next piece. Keep working!

Chapter 1: Learning the Piece

Don't be in a hurry to put away the score before you are really, truly ready to memorize. Playing very well *with* the music is the best foundation for playing well from memory. As you practice, think about which sections you expect will be easier to memorize, and which sections will be difficult. You or your teacher have probably developed a method of practice by which you solidify notes and rhythms, but there are other practice habits that are especially appropriate for music that you intend to memorize at some point.

Try the methods described in this chapter, but don't hesitate to make up your own methods as well. Think outside of the box. The more unique ways you can think of to practice your piece, the more you are challenging yourself, making your command of the music stronger.

After you have learned your piece and can play it quite effortlessly with the score, you are ready to start memorizing. But you first have to reach that point.

Work in Small Sections

An entire page of music is too much for your brain to take in at once. Pick a short section, no more than 4 to 8 measures, and work on *just that* until you see measurable progress.

You don't have to work on the whole piece every time you practice. The most productive practice sessions usually involve a run-through or two, to keep the piece under your fingers and to make you aware of the sections that are the weakest, and then a good amount of practice focused on just a few short sections.

Understand Your Piece on an Intellectual Level

Study the score and look for patterns. Don't be afraid to mark up the sheet music! Photocopy the score if you want to preserve a clean version.

As you study the score, group the music into phrases, or complete musical ideas. Be sure that your phrases make musical sense, and that the end of the phrase comes at a place that sounds and feels right for the piece. Memorizing a series of phrases is much easier than memorizing note by note. It's just like memorizing a speech - it is easier when you think in complete sentences, rather than trying to memorize individual letters!

Number the phrases in your score. This will be useful for practicing with the score, and more useful still once you start to focus on memorization.

Know What Material is Repeated, and Where

When you identify repeated material, you are also identifying areas where previous memory can assist new memory. As a visual aid, you might even want to highlight repeated sections in the same color. If material is not repeated exactly but is slightly altered, take note of what the similarities and differences are.

Practice the Scales and Arpeggios for the Key of the Piece

Scale passages and chordal passages appear *all the time* in music; more often than you have probably realized. You will be shocked at how much of an impact mastering the scale and arpeggio of the same key can have on your piece.

As you practice scales and arpeggios, watch for passages in your piece that use them. Also notice if the piece has any scale or arpeggio passages in different keys. If it does, practice those scales and arpeggios as well.

Practice Everything with a Metronome

Use a metronome, starting with a beat slow enough that you can play the phrase perfectly almost every time. At each metronome mark, repeat a short section until it's easy to play at that tempo. This should be done at least 5 to 10 times. When you can play the phrase perfectly most of the time, increase the metronome speed by one or two ticks, and repeat the process.

Play the Same Way Every Time

Be very particular about fingerings, bowings, breaths, articulations, and any other details of performance that need to be planned ahead of time. If you sometimes play the same passage in different ways, your brain doesn't know which way to do it, and gets confused when you try to reconstruct the passage from memory.

Decide on fingering, bowing, and breaths in the very beginning, before you do a lot of work on the piece. Be as logical as possible in these decisions. Try to come up with a technique that makes the passage easy to play, and that also gets musical results. Material that is repeated exactly or slightly altered later in the piece should be fingered/bowed/phrased the same way. If you have a private teacher, or if you know any more experienced musicians, they can offer you a lot of help in this area.

After you make decisions about these performance details, *pencil them in your score so you can be sure you are being consistent.* Most importantly, stick to these decisions *religiously.* During practice, an incorrect fingering, bowing, or breath is just as bad as a wrong note or rhythm – You have to go back right then and fix it.

Chapter 2: Starting to Memorize

The ease of memorizing a piece depends on how proficiently you can play the piece with the score. There is just *no substitute* for this foundation. Make double sure that all the technical and musical kinks have been worked out before you even think about memorizing!

Go to your instrument and try to play through your whole piece, cold. Use the sheet music. If you make even one mistake, spend your practice time that day fixing that mistake before you spend it on memorizing. Don't cut corners.

Once you can play your whole piece perfectly the very first time through, you are ready to start memorizing. You should always feel free to use practice time to work with your sheet music, ironing out any issues that come up.

If you've never successfully memorized a piece of music before, take a moment to prepare yourself for the new challenge that lies ahead. Even if you have memorized before, reading this section might give you new insight into things you have already experienced. Memorization practice is different from note learning, so keep that in mind. You already know the notes, so simply doing run-throughs of the piece over and over again is not really an effective use of your practice time. You need to focus using your time on making measurable progress towards playing the whole piece from memory.

Preparation

Different challenges in memorization will arise from the specific piece you are playing, your instrument, and your own strengths and weaknesses as a musician. Think about the obstacles you can expect to face as you memorize. Does your piece have irregular rhythms, or a lot of accidentals and passages outside the key? How much material in the piece is repeated or similar? Are there a lot of passages that just don't "fall under the fingers?" Does the piece flow logically from beginning to end, or are there a lot of surprises and "twists"?

What about you, the musician? Is the piece at the higher end of your technical ability? Have you ever played music like this before? Ever memorized music like this before? If so, what was easy and what was hard for you then? Finally, do you "feel" the piece, and have an emotional connection to what you are playing?

"Getting" Your Piece

As you work, you will probably find that the sections that are easiest to memorize are exactly the same sections that evoke the most emotion in you. This is no coincidence. Having an emotional connection to the music means that you "get it"; the musical statement makes sense to you, it *means* something. In music, *meaning* is much easier to memorize than nonsense, just like a meaningful sentence is easier to memorize than a string of random words.

On the other side of the coin, those passages that you "don't get" or that aren't emotional for you will be much harder to memorize (or to play at all, for that matter). Identify these passages in your piece. Spend some of your practice time each day scrutinizing these sections, and trying to see and hear them from a different perspective.

Some of this can be done at your instrument. Try playing the sections in a new way, listening and thinking about what you like and what you don't like. Try different dynamics, some rubato, different articulation, or making certain notes more emphatic than you usually do. You might just fall into something that makes sense to you.

There is also some work to be done away from your instrument. Read your score, and try to imagine listening to the piece exactly as you think it should sound. This lets you be musically creative without getting bogged down in the technicalities of actually playing your instrument.

Finally, listen to recordings of the piece if there are any available. If any of your instrument's great performers chose to record this piece, you can be sure they "got it," and listening to them just might open up your ears. It can also be extremely enlightening to hear how your part interacts with the other parts or with the accompaniment, if this applies to your piece.

To see the value in these exercises, all you have to do is look at how much easier it is to memorize those passages that are especially emotional for you. It's clear that developing the same kind of connection to the more difficult passages would immediately make them significantly easier to memorize, and potentially save you a number of hours of practice. So don't question whether practice time can be well spent away from your instrument.

How Memorization Happens

The work you need to do to memorize a piece is very different than the work you do in learning to play the piece. Playing notes, rhythms, articulations, breaths, dynamics... these are all things that you just have to train your hands, arms, lips, and lungs to do correctly when prompted. Instrumental practice is essentially a physical task.

However, memorization happens in your *brain*, not in your hands. Hours and hours of chugging away at your instrument without being mentally engaged will be no help towards your goal of playing from memory. You may develop "muscle memory" in this way, but playing from "muscle memory" alone is likely to be very insecure, and can never be musical.

When you play memorized music, your brain is accessing information it got through touch, sound, and sight.

When you practiced with the sheet music, you taught your brain, *"how it feels"* to play the piece on your instrument; *"how the piece sounds"*; and *what the score "looks like."* Therefore, when your brain recalls this information, you are using three different types of memory: *Tactile* memory, *aural* memory, and *visual* memory.

The more solid all three types of memory are and the more connections you can build between each type of memory, the less likely it is that your memory will fail during a performance. When you plan your memorization practice, make sure that you choose a variety of practice methods that will address all three different types of memory. Some examples are given here. They will be explained more thoroughly in later sections.

Tactile Memory

To use and practice tactile memory:

- Remember how it feels to play your piece.
- Practice at your instrument. Try to play a short section with the music, then a few times without.
- "Shadow" practice by making the same motions that you would make to play the piece, except without your instrument in hand. This can be done with or without your sheet music.

Aural Memory

To use and practice aural memory:

- Remember what your piece sounds like.
- Listen to recordings of your piece. If no recordings of professional musicians are available, record yourself playing the piece and listen to that.
- Read your score, but sing or hum the piece instead of playing it on your instrument. If you have two different parts at the same time, like in songs for piano and some songs for strings, you can break it into individual voices that can be sung – for example, sing the right hand part, then sing the left hand part.

Visual Memory

To use and practice visual memory:

- Remember what the score looks like.
- Practice without the sheet music, but try to picture the notes as they appear on the page. Sometimes it helps to refresh your memory by playing a short section a couple of times with the music, then take the score away and trying to picture what you just saw.
- Study your score. Read the notes straight through, in rhythm, but don't play your

instrument or hum. Take note of details like articulation marks, dynamic marks, breath marks, bowings, fingerings, etc.

Micro- and Macro- Level Memorization

In addition to using three different senses to memorize, your brain also memorizes on two different temporal levels. To make it all the way through a piece, you must *always* know what note comes next and what section comes next.

Knowing what note comes next is micro-level, or small-scale memory. While you are playing from memory, you need to know what happens in the immediate future, so that you can send your hands and fingers to the right place.

Knowing what section comes next is macro-level, or large-scale memory. To be able to connect one section with the next in a musical way, you need to know what the next section is. A solid macro-level memory lets you miss a note here and there without the whole piece falling apart.

When you practice to memorize, make sure you are always aware of the next note *and* the next section. Even if you're not going to practice the next section right then, being aware of what it is will help your macro-level memory.

Macro-memory is more important than micro-memory in a lot of ways, but it can't really be made useful without first developing a solid micro-memory. You can know the form of your piece and the order of the sections backwards and forwards, but if you can't play the notes of any of those sections... well, you can't even start your piece, let alone make it all the way through from memory.

With that in mind, it is a good idea to start your memorization practice with your focus on micro-memorizing.

Chapter 3: Micro-memorization

The most important thing to watch for when you memorize note by note is that you don't try to stuff too much into your brain at one time. If you can stay focused enough and spend your entire practice time for a day on just a measure or two, it's possible that you will never have to practice those measures again. Instead of trying to memorize a whole lot of music in one practice session, try to make what you *do* memorize as solid as possible. Make your practice time count!

Before you start practicing, decide on your goal for that practice session. Set your sights reasonably, and once you achieve your goal, take a break! *Sleep is your friend.*

During a practice section:

1. Once you've picked out a short section (usually 1 to 4 bars long), start working on it methodically. Play through it several times with the music. Take note of what dynamics and articulation is has. Make sure you use the correct fingering, bowing, and so forth. Next, set your instrument aside and look for patterns in the section. What is the shape of the melody; does it go up and come back down, or go down and come back up? Is the melody constructed of steps, skips, or both? Do the notes fit within a certain scale or arpeggio that

you know? What is the rhythm - quarter notes, eighths, sixteenths, or a mixture? Are any notes or rhythms repeated?

2. After you answer these questions and discover the patterns in the section, play it a few more times with the sheet music, thinking about the structure you now understand as you play.

3. Sometimes the act of focusing on a small section, understanding it intellectually, and practicing it in isolation will be enough to make it "stick" in your brain. Try it now to see if this is the case. Take a last look at your score, find the first note of the section, then close your eyes and try to play what you just worked on. If you can play it from memory, keep doing so several times in a row. If you slip, try starting from the beginning of the section before you look at the score. Think about the patterns you recognized earlier; they will help you remember what comes next.

If the section hasn't "stuck" yet, do some more methodical practice. First, try just repeating steps 1 to 4. You might be rushing your brain without realizing it. Or, try taking a small portion of the section you're working on. The fewer notes there are, the easier it will be to memorize. But if the section is still not sticking, you may need to try something different.

Recitation

Following your score, recite the note names one by one (e.g., "D, G, A, B, C, D, G, G"). Don't worry about the rhythm yet. As you recite, sing the melody, or finger along on your instrument, or both. Then start reciting from memory. This is easy to do, and you're not busting your chops, so do it a whole bunch of times in a row. Keep reciting and fingering until it's boring and your mind starts to wander.

Next, do the rhythm, without worrying about the notes. Following your score, clap or tap the rhythm of the melody. If the melody is catchy you might be able to hum along, but if not, that's okay. Then, start to clap or tap without looking at the music. Again, this is easy to do, and you're not busting your chops, so keep repeating it until it's so easy that your mind starts to wander.

If saying the notes or clapping the rhythm by itself never gets easier (you always have to focus hard to get it right), then you probably have taken too large a section to memorize at one time. Try cutting the section in half and starting over.

Now that you have spent time on the rhythm, you might have forgotten the note names. Go back and refresh. Then, once you've spent time on the note names, you might have forgotten the rhythm, so go back and refresh... When have gone back and forth several times, drilling note names and rhythms separately, try putting them together. Don't play yet, just recite the note names in rhythm, and hum the melody or finger your instrument along with the rhythm, if you can. Do this until it gets boring and your mind starts to wander. All of this work should be done at first with the score, then without it when you are able.

Try playing it on your instrument, very slowly. Recite the note names in your head, as you were just doing, and then find that note on your instrument. As you repeat the section and gain confidence, try to find some of the notes without first reciting their names in your head, and gradually increase the tempo.

Has it clicked yet? If so, repeat the section several times, listening to yourself and trying to picture the score (without actually looking at it). The more you repeat the section and the more mentally engaged you are, the more you are solidifying the three senses of memorization: touch, sound, and sight.

Even once you memorize the section and have played it several times in a row, your memory might seem suddenly to disappear. This is okay; just go back to the score for a bit to refresh. You might need to recite note names or clap rhythms a couple of times again. Don't get discouraged; building a solid memory of music takes time and patience.

Tricky Sections

If you are having significant trouble with a particular section, you might need to slow way, way down, and literally memorize note by note. Make sure the section you are working with is short enough for your brain to take in this way; probably only 1 or 2 measures, perhaps even less than a measure it has a lot of notes.

Start by playing your very short section a few times with the score. Then, play *just* the first note, then the last note. Skip everything in the middle. Take time in between the two notes (take a breath, lift your bow - whatever you need to do). Now play *just those two notes*, the first note and the last note, from memory. It's only two notes, you can do it!

Between the time you play the first note and the last note, while you take to breathe or lift your bow or your hands, try to imagine the sound of the rest of the phrase. You don't have to remember the names of the notes, or find them on your instrument. Just imagine the general shape and rhythm of the melody that lies in between your first and last note. Simultaneously, stay focused on that last note that you have to hit.

Stick with just the first and last note for a good while. If you ever have trouble imagining the rest of the phrase, go back and play all the notes from the score, listening to the sound of the section.

Once you can start the phrase by playing the first note, clearly hear the rest of the notes in your imagination, and then end by playing the last note without hesitation, you are ready to start adding more notes. Don't rush through this. Always build a solid foundation before trying to memorize more.

The next note to add is the second-to-last. So you will be playing the first note, pausing while you imagine the rest of the phrase, and then playing the last *two* notes. Do it a couple times with the score, then without. It's only three notes, and you already memorized two of them. You can do it!

Continue to add one note at a time, either at the start or the end of the phrase. As you fill in more and more of the notes in the middle, you'll start to understand how the beginning of the phrase connects with the end. Take your time, and don't feel that you necessarily have to get to all the notes in a single practice session. Just stick with this one short section until you get it. Once you do have all the notes memorized, make sure to play the section several times through to solidify it.

Memorization Takes Time and Persistence

You've worked hard, focused intently on only a very short section, and can see results in just one practice session. Finding that you have a part of your piece solidly memorized, even if it's a very short part, is a huge confidence boost. Enjoy it now, but be warned: the bulk of your work still lies ahead.

In fact, you may put your instrument down today, and pick it up tomorrow and feel like your memory of the section you worked on is gone. Don't despair. Try going through the memorization process on that section again. You will probably find that "rememorizing" the same section will only take a fraction of the time that it took to memorize it the first time.

This is where careful planning of your memorization practice comes in. You can't spend time every practice session rememorizing everything you have already worked on; you won't have time left over to memorize anything new! You need to find a balance between memorizing new material and reinforcing memory of material you have already worked on.

Making a Memorization Plan

Make memorizing every individual section of the piece, at least in the short term, a priority; that is, go through the steps above, until you're able to play one section confidently from memory at the end of your practice session. Each day, set your goal (just one or two sections that are one to four bars long) and learn the notes. As you learn what memorization methods work best for you, and as you develop more confidence in your ability to memorize, the amount of time it takes to memorize one of these short sections will decrease. You might also run into material that is similar or identical to something you already worked on, which will of course be easier to memorize. After you accomplish the goal you set, use any time you have left over to reinforce the sections you worked on previously.

Rememorizing is the same as memorizing: your brain can only take in so much. Don't try to take longer sections or connect sections together yet. Stick with one short section at a time. First play it from the score a few times; think about the underlying patterns you've found; then try to play without the score. The first few times you rememorize, you might have to go back to reciting note names or adding note by note. Remain determined and do what you have to do. When you can play the section correctly 5 to 10 times in a row, without the score, you have it rememorized and you can move on and rememorize the next section.

When your note-by-note memorization is confident enough that you can individually rememorize every section of your piece inside the time of one practice session, you are ready begin macro-memorizing, or connecting the sections together.

Chapter 4: Macro-memorization

Macro-memorization is all about connecting together the short sections that you know. In all of your practices so far, you have taken time between short sections to refresh your memory of the next section before playing it. If you want to be able to play the whole song, you need to be able to recall your knowledge of every section without a refresher.

Effective macro-memorization, just like micro-memorization, comes from practicing a whole lot, and using a variety of practice methods. Make sure you don't rely too heavily on just one type of memory. For example, if your only practice methods are constant repetition and shadow practicing, you might be relying too heavily on "muscle memory," or the memory of what it feels like to play the piece. But, at the same time, if you never practice either of those ways, you might not be developing your muscle memory enough. Always strive for a balance between memory based on touch, sound, and sight.

The methods listed below are a few methods for macro-memorization that are known to work for practicing musicians. Not every method works well for everybody, but it is definitely a good idea to try all of them out, especially if you are new to memorizing. Find out what works for you.

The methods are listed in no particular order. Try mixing them up, and come back to any method that worked for you after try a few others.

Remember: More hours of practice, by itself, does *not* necessarily lead to better memorization. Practicing in a variety of ways, and making sure you are well-rested and mentally engaged while you practice, will ensure the most efficient use of your time.

Constant Repetition

This method is very much like what you did to micro-memorize. The only difference is that the goal is to gradually increase the length of the sections that you can play at one time. A metronome is a great aid to this method.

Take the first and the second short sections of your piece together. Set the metronome on a low speed that forces you to concentrate and that makes the passage technically easy to play. Because of the micro-memorization work you have done, you should be able to make it to the end of the first short section without a problem. The challenge will be transitioning from the first to the second section.

Try playing the first section from memory, and then looking at the score to get your bearings for the second section. Then, try watching the score for the first section, but looking away and playing from memory once you get to the beginning of the second section.

Try *imagining* playing the first section (without looking at the score), and then actually play the second section – without hesitating or peeking in between. Look at your score, and study the way the two sections connect together. It might help to play the last couple of notes of the first section and the first couple of notes of the second section together, from memory.

However you do it, you need to eventually play both the first and second sections together from memory. Once you can do this, turn your metronome on to that slow tempo. Repeat those two sections until you have made the transition seamlessly at least 5 or 10 times. Then, increase the metronome by one or two ticks (no more!) and do the same work. Continue increasing the metronome (always gradually) until you reach your final tempo. By that point, you will probably have done dozens of repetitions of the two sections. Ideally, your hands will just start to go to the right place without you having to think too hard about it. You are developing muscle memory.

Next, do the same work on the second and the third sections. Don't jump straight to the third and fourth sections – you'll leave a "gap" at the transition between the second and third where you won't have practiced from memory.

Once you've gone through the whole piece, in 2-section chunks, go on to a different practice method for a while. If you choose to come back to this method, then you can work in larger chunks; three or perhaps four sections at a time.

Study the score

No matter how much you've analyzed and how many patterns you've unearthed in your piece, chances are that there are more patterns still for you to discover. Even very experienced musicians often underestimate the power of studying the score. Composers don't just throw notes on a page, they try to create something that makes sense. If you can better understand how the pieces fit together, your memory will be stronger, and your playing will also be more musical.

You should also try to read the score straight through from beginning to end, without your instrument, and imagine hearing the piece being played, or playing it yourself at your instrument, or both. Take note of passages where your imagination seems to falter. These are the sections that probably need more practice.

If you really want to challenge your knowledge of your score, try getting a blank piece of manuscript paper and writing the whole piece out, note by note. You can go to your instrument and play to remind yourself of the notes, but don't cheat and look at the score!

Listen to Your Piece

Listening to your piece is one of the best ways to take in the big picture, and to understand how one section or pattern leads to another. If you can find recordings of professional musicians playing your piece, that's great. If not, a cheap microphone and your own rendition (with the help of your score) will do the trick.

When you listen, don't always focus your mind on the same aspects of the piece each time. Listening to your piece without really focusing on it is a good way to get it into your subconscious and build your aural memory. Because this doesn't require any mental effort, you should be able to do it frequently. Put the song on repeat while you do chores or exercise. Listen once or twice before you go to bed. If you are trying to memorize a piece of music, it's advantageous to have it "stuck in your head."

You can also use your recording to build connections between your aural memory and the other types of memory. Listen while you follow along in your score. Try starting the recording in the middle and see how fast you can find your place in the music.

To build connections between aural memory and tactile (muscle) memory, listen and play along or finger your instrument. This can also help you improve your phrasing and dynamics, if you learn to imitate a professional player. But don't lose sight of your own interpretation either.

Shadow Practice

This type of practice involves taking away all of the visual and aural cues, and some of the tactile cues you are used to having. Without your sheet music and without your instrument, go through the same movements you would make to play the piece. Try to hear the song in your head. Do this both while humming or singing along and without.

You can also give yourself some of the tactile cues that you are used to, without actually playing your instrument. Pianists can "play" on a tabletop. String players can pick up their bow but not their instrument. String and wind players can finger on their instrument without blowing into the mouthpiece or bowing. Pretending to play your instrument is already a stretch for your imagination, so if you can make it all the way through your piece at the same time, you know your memory is in good shape.

Practice Running the Piece

When you finally do perform your piece in public, you will be nervous. Your brain will be working differently than it did while you practiced. Even if you have played the piece a thousand times correctly from memory, it's possible that in the heat of the moment you will have a slip.

So be prepared to slip! This means that, while you're practicing running the piece from memory, don't ever stop to fix a mistake. If at all possible, just play right through it like nothing happened at all. If it throws off your memory, jump *ahead* to a place that you can remember. Don't ever jump backwards and try to play the same thing again, because there's a good chance you'll slip up at the same place you did before. This can send you into a "stop-and-start" loop where you make the same mistake, go back a measure or two, and then play that measure or two and make the same mistake again, over and over! If this happens in a performance it will totally derail your confidence, and distract the audience. So, don't let yourself get in the habit of practicing like this. Note that this is different from the advice given for micro-memorization; during micro-memorization, you are learning the notes, and fixing mistakes is critical so you memorize the correct notes in the right order. During macro-memorization, you're learning to connect the sections, so your focus should be on the flow of section to section.

You might need to prepare "signpost" sections, places where you know your memory is so confident that you can jump straight there from anywhere in the piece, and play it perfectly any time. Mark these in your score. Practice randomly jumping to these signpost sections during your run-throughs, and see if you can make it to the end.

While you're doing your run-through, try to keep a mental record of the places where your memory slips so that you can come back to them and solidify those sections. It might be too difficult for you to focus on playing the piece and remembering past slips at the same time. If so, try recording yourself during run-throughs so you have a definite record of what slipped.

Solidify the Ending

If you always start from the beginning and practice until you hit an extremely rough spot, then focus exclusively on that rough spot, the ending of your piece will be neglected. Do some of your memorization work backwards – start with the last phrase at the end of the piece, then work towards the beginning, gradually adding on more phrases. Then, while you're performing, your memory and confidence will only get stronger and stronger as the piece goes on.

You should also be able to start your piece at any place in the middle, and make it all the way to the end. Just pick a random measure out of your score, start there, and try to make it all the way to the end. Don't stop for anything, but take note of where you slip so you can go back and solidify those spots. Don't choose the same starting measure twice in a row.

Let Your Brain Do Its Thing

If you're going to memorize music, you have to work *with* your brain, not against it. Be aware of which practice methods are working for you and which aren't, and try to figure out why some are more effective. Analyze your own psychology. What conditions brought about your most productive practice sessions? Perhaps they were at a certain time of day, or in a certain room? When you practice, do you retain what you learned to the next day?

While you practice you should always, always, always be mentally engaged and positive. Your brain simply does not learn if you are too tired, or if you try to do too much at one time, or if you get frustrated or angry at your music, your instrument, or yourself. If you start to make more errors than usual, don't take that as a sign that you need to practice harder or push yourself more. Take it as a sign that you *need a break*, and then take that break. Take a nap, step away from your instrument, or at least practice something else for a few minutes. Come back to the difficult passage only when you feel fresh.

If you can, add a short practice right before bed. It will only take 10 minutes or so to quickly review everything you covered that day, and it will help you in being able to do the same thing tomorrow.

At some point you will start to feel that your piece is very solidly memorized. Now is the time to challenge yourself. Instead of just playing over and over and over, find out which type of memory is weakest and work on solidifying it. Remember that if all three types of memory are strong, if you get nervous and lose one during your performance you will still have two to rely on. It pays to diversify.

Warning! Only do these final "testing" exercises when your memory is really, really strong. You should be able to play the whole piece through, without refreshing your memory by looking at the score. You should be playing the correct notes and rhythms, with the correct fingerings, bowings, etc, every time. If you try to challenge your memory while it is not solid, you can end up confusing yourself and actually do more harm than good.

Practice Starting and Stopping

Play up to a spot in the middle of the piece, then just stop. Go do something else, or practice another song for a few minutes. Then try to come back and pick up exactly where you left off. Also, try starting in the middle of the piece and making it through all the way to end.

Slow It Down

Chances are that your memory has started to drift into the "subconscious" as you practice. You can play through without any mistakes, but you are not really aware of each and every note, and every movement you have to make. This is dangerous! When you perform, you're going to get nervous, and your subconscious is going to be distracted by that. You need to make sure your piece is solidly memorized on a more conscious level, so that you have something to rely on. It is important to practice forcing yourself to play from consciousness instead of by rote memory.

Start by playing your piece at its performance tempo. Find the metronome mark that matches that, and go a tick or two lower.

Now, start doing run-throughs with the metronome. Every time you successfully make it to the end of your piece, *decrease* the metronome's tempo by a tick. As it gets slower and slower, you'll feel your subconscious muscle memory start to falter. Even though you are going slower and slower, it gets harder and harder to find the notes in time!

Go back to review the score as needed. Keep decreasing the tempo with each successful run-through until you are able to play it through at half speed with the metronome on.

Intentionally Throw Yourself Off, Then Try to Recover

If you plan it right, you can mess up your run-through worse than anything that could ever happen in a real performance. If you can learn to recover from these planned disasters, something as insignificant as a wrong note during your performance won't even faze you.

Start on the wrong note, or play the first phrase in the wrong rhythm or with the wrong articulation. Then try to get back on track in the second phrase.

Randomly skip a section. Try to play through seamlessly, as if it had been written that way originally. Don't skip the same section two run-throughs in a row.

Randomly repeat a section. Same idea as above.

Sabotage your instrument. On a violin or cello you might detune one string. On a wind instrument you could put your reed on a little crooked. On a piano you could tape two keys together. Try to play the piece through as if nothing is wrong. (If something like this should ever come up in an actual performance it is probably more appropriate to fix the problem before you start playing, if possible. This is just a test.)

Try playing the piece without warming up, at all. Imagine you got stuck in traffic and as soon as you get to the venue you have to run out on stage.

Be creative! Think about what else could possibly go wrong, and prepare for that.

The more you test yourself and pass, the more solid your memory will be, and the better chance you have for a truly remarkable performance from memory. Keep your eyes on the prize, and good luck!

Recommended Resources

- HowExpert.com – Quick 'How To' Guides on All Topics from A to Z by Everyday Experts.
- HowExpert.com/free – Free HowExpert Email Newsletter.
- HowExpert.com/books – HowExpert Books
- HowExpert.com/courses – HowExpert Courses
- HowExpert.com/clothing – HowExpert Clothing
- HowExpert.com/membership – HowExpert Membership Site
- HowExpert.com/affiliates – HowExpert Affiliate Program
- HowExpert.com/writers – Write About Your #1 Passion/Knowledge/Expertise & Become a HowExpert Author.
- HowExpert.com/resources – Additional HowExpert Recommended Resources
- YouTube.com/HowExpert – Subscribe to HowExpert YouTube.
- Instagram.com/HowExpert – Follow HowExpert on Instagram.
- Facebook.com/HowExpert – Follow HowExpert on Facebook.

Made in the USA
Coppell, TX
13 September 2020